A-Z of
DINOSAURS

A TEMPLAR BOOK

British Library Cataloguing in Publication Data
is available for this title

ISBN 0 340 55761 3 cased
ISBN 0 340 55762 1 limp

Copyright © The Templar Company plc 1990
Illustrations copyright © The Templar Company plc 1990

First published 1990 by Derrydale Books, New York, USA
First published in Great Britain 1991

All rights reserved. No part of this publication may be reproduced or
transmitted in any form or by any means, electronically or mechanically,
including photocopying, recording, or any information storage and retrieval
system, without either prior permission in writing from the publisher or a
licence permitting restricted copying. In the United Kingdom such licences
are issued by the Copyright Licensing Agency, 90 Tottenham Court Road,
London W1P 9HE.

Published by Hodder and Stoughton Children's Books,
a division of Hodder and Stoughton Ltd,
Mill Road, Dunton Green, Sevenoaks, Kent TN13 2YA

Devised and produced by The Templar Company plc,
Pippbrook Mill, London Road, Dorking, Surrey RH4 1JE

Editor Andy Charman
Designer Sue Rawkins

Colour separation by Positive Colour Ltd, Maldon, Essex

Printed in Malaysia

A-Z of DINOSAURS

Written by
Anita Ganeri

Illustrated by
Tessa Hamilton

HODDER AND STOUGHTON
LONDON SYDNEY AUCKLAND TORONTO

What were the dinosaurs?

The mighty dinosaurs first appeared on Earth about 220 million years ago. They were reptiles, like the crocodiles and turtles found today. There were many different kinds of dinosaurs, from huge, slow plant-eaters to fierce, fast meat-eaters. Dinosaurs ruled the Earth for about 160 million years, about 80 times longer than human beings have lived on Earth. About 65 million years ago the dinosaurs died out. No one is sure why this happened. One idea is that small mammals stole the dinosaurs' eggs. Other people think that the Earth became colder at that time. The dinosaurs may have starved or frozen to death.

Although no one has ever seen dinosaurs, we know a lot about them from fossils. Fossils are the hard parts of a dinosaur's body, such as its bones and teeth. When a dinosaur died, its body was buried by layers and layers of rock and mud. Over millions of years its bones turned to stone. Fossils are found in places where the weather has worn the rocks away or where the rocks have broken. Fossils have to be removed very carefully because they are so delicate. The first fossil bone was found more than 300 years ago. At the time, people thought it belonged to a giant man. They had no idea that dinosaurs had ever existed.

A

The forests of 70 million years ago were dangerous places. Plant-eating dinosaurs, such as **Anatosaurus**, were always on the look-out for fierce hunters. One of the most terrible of these was **Albertosaurus**. It was a fast runner and had very sharp teeth.

Flying about in the tree tops 150 million years ago was **Archaeopteryx**. This early bird had teeth and lived on insects and lizards.

Archaeopteryx
(Ar-kee-op-ter-icks)

Albertosaurus
(Al-ber-tow-saw-rus)

Anatosaurus
(An-at-owe-saw-rus)

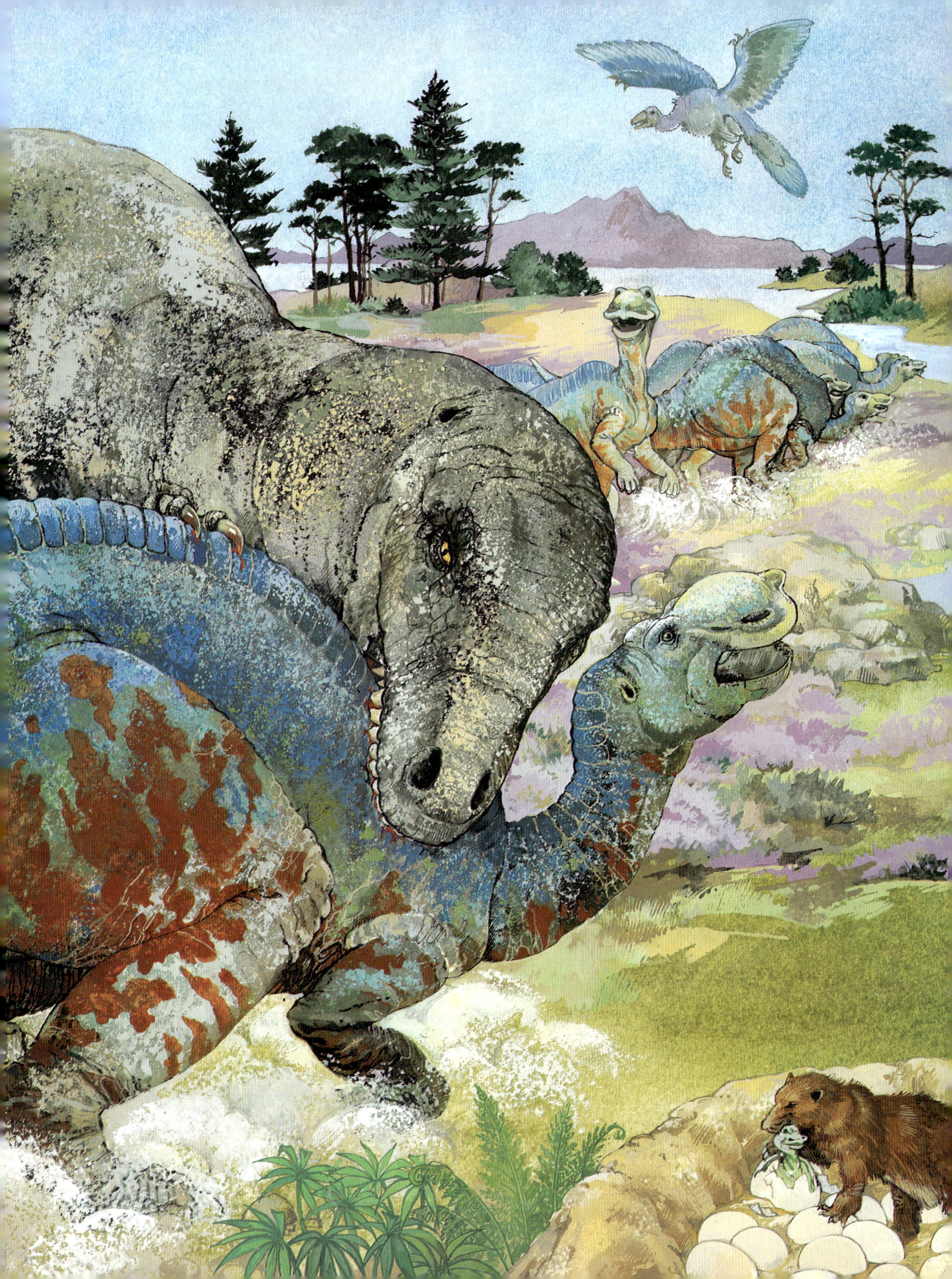

B

Brachiosaurus
(Brack-e-owe-saw-rus)

Plateosaurus
(Plat-ee-owe-saw-rus)

The gigantic **Brachiosaurus** was the heaviest dinosaur of all. It weighed about 80 tonnes, as much as 15 elephants. It had a huge body and was taller than a house. Brachiosaurus lived in Africa about 140 million years ago. It used its long neck to pluck leaves from the highest tree tops, as a giraffe does today.

Plateosaurus, **Camarasaurus** and **Euskelosaurus** also used their long necks to reach their food.

Camarasaurus
(Cam-ar-ah-saw-rus)

Euskelosaurus
(You-skel-owe-saw-rus)

C

Not all dinosaurs were giants. **Compsognathus** was only about the size of a chicken and was one of the smallest dinosaurs that ever lived. **Coelurus** was under 2 metres tall, with a head the size of a person's hand. **Coelophysis** was nearly 2,000 times lighter than Brachiosaurus!

These three dinosaurs were meat-eaters and fast hunters. They darted about on their back legs, searching for lizards to eat. They also used their speed to run away from hungry enemies.

Coelophysis
(See-low-fizz-is)

Camarasaurus
(Cam-ar-ah-saw-rus)

Coelurus
(See-loo-rus)

Compsognathus
(Comp-sog-nay-thus)

11

D

Diplodocus lived about 140 million years ago, in North America. It measured an amazing 28 metres from its tiny head to the tip of its whip-like tail. This is longer than a line of eight cars parked bumper to bumper and makes Diplodocus one of the longest dinosaurs that ever lived. Diplodocus had quite a slim body, though, weighing only about 10 tonnes.

Diplodocus was a plant-eater but it had weak teeth and couldn't chew its food. Instead, it had a special stomach for grinding leaves.

Diplodocus
(Dip-lod-owe-cus)

Coelurus
(See-loo-rus)

E

Edmontosaurus
(Ed-mon-tow-saw-rus)

Elasmosaurus
(Ell-as-mow-saw-rus)

Euoplocephalus
(You-owe-plo-keff-al-us)

From about 136 to 65 million years ago, hundreds of kinds of dinosaurs lived all over the world. This is called the Cretaceous period. **Edmontosaurus** was a huge plant-eater and one of the last dinosaurs to live on Earth. **Euoplocephalus** was built like a tank. Thick, bony plates protected its body and at the end of its tail was a huge club which it could swing at its enemies. In the sea, lived a long-necked reptile called **Elasmosaurus**. This creature was a close relative of the dinosaurs.

F, G

Not all dinosaurs were slow and clumsy. **Fabrosaurus** was a small, light plant-eater that lived 210 million years ago in South Africa. It could run very quickly on its long back legs. **Gallimimus** was another speedy dinosaur. Holding its long tail out for balance, it could run nearly as fast as a racehorse. Gallimimus lived about 65 million years ago in central Asia.

Fabrosaurus
(Fab-row-saw-rus)

Gallimimus
(Gal-ee-my-mus)

Ostrich dinosaurs

Ostrich

Gallimimus is known as an ostrich dinosaur. This is because it looked like a featherless version of a modern-day ostrich.

17

H We can learn a lot about how dinosaurs lived from the fossil clues left in the rocks. Dinosaur teeth make good fossils because they are hard and do not decay. Scientists study the fossil teeth and compare them to the teeth of animals living today. This tells them how the dinosaurs lived and what they ate. Plant-eaters usually had flat, blunt teeth. Meat-eaters had sharp, dagger-like teeth.

Heterodontosaurus
(Heta-row-don-tow-saw-rus)

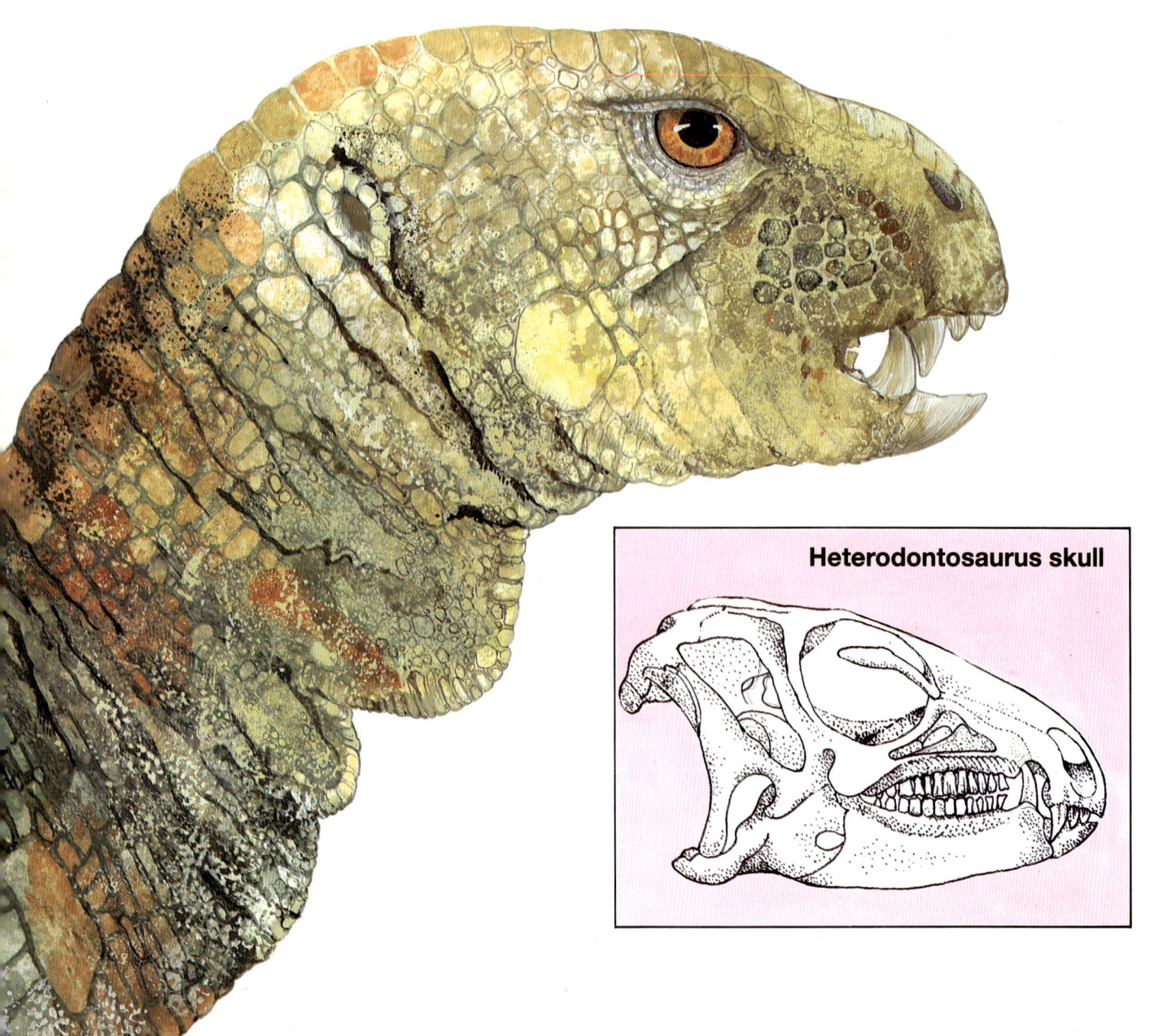

Heterodontosaurus skull

Hypsilophodon
(Hip-sill-off-owe-don)

Most dinosaurs had just one type of tooth, but the plant-eating **Heterodontosaurus** was very unusual. Its name means "reptile with mixed teeth". Its front teeth were small and sharp. Behind these it had tusk-like teeth and at the back of its jaw it had flat teeth for grinding. This small dinosaur lived 220 million years ago in South Africa. **Hypsilophodon's** name means "high-ridged tooth". Its teeth had special folds, or ridges, for munching fruit. It lived 130 million years ago in Europe.

I

Iguanodon lived about 120 million years ago in Europe, Africa and Asia. In 1877, some 31 Iguanodon skeletons were found in a coal mine in Belgium. They showed that these 11-metre-long dinosaurs may have lived in large herds.

Iguanodon walked on its back legs, leaving its hands free for grabbing plants. Its spiky thumbs may have been used as weapons.

Iguanodon
(Ig-you-ah-no-don)

Dinosaur feet

Like today's elephants, Diplodocus had huge, squat feet to bear the weight of its massive body.

Compsognathus had long, bird-like feet, showing that it was a very fast runner.

Iguandon's three-toed feet were big to support its large body. They also allowed it to run quickly.

J, K

Like most reptiles today, dinosaurs such as **Kentrosaurus** and **Jubbulpuria** laid eggs. The eggs had tough shells and the dinosaurs laid them in nests dug out of the soft ground. Then the eggs were covered in sand to keep them warm until the baby dinosaurs hatched out.

Kronosaurus was a huge, prehistoric sea-living reptile. It may have dragged itself out of the water to lay its eggs on land.

Kentrosaurus
(Ken-trow-saw-rus)

Jubbulpuria
(Jubb-ull-pew-ree-ah)

Kronosaurus
(Kron-ow-saw-rus)

L

Many dinosaurs had oddly-shaped heads and mouths. **Lesothosaurus** was about the size of a duck. It had a sharp beak for snipping off leaves and shoots. **Lambeosaurus** had a huge, hollow crest on its head. It may have blown the crest like a trumpet to tell other dinosaurs where it was. **Leptoceratops** had a frill round its neck. It belonged to the group known as horned dinosaurs, although it had no horns!

Leptoceratops
(Lep-tow-sir-ah-tops)

Lesothosaurus
(Less-oo-too-saw-rus)

Lambeosaurus
(Lam-be-owe-saw-rus)

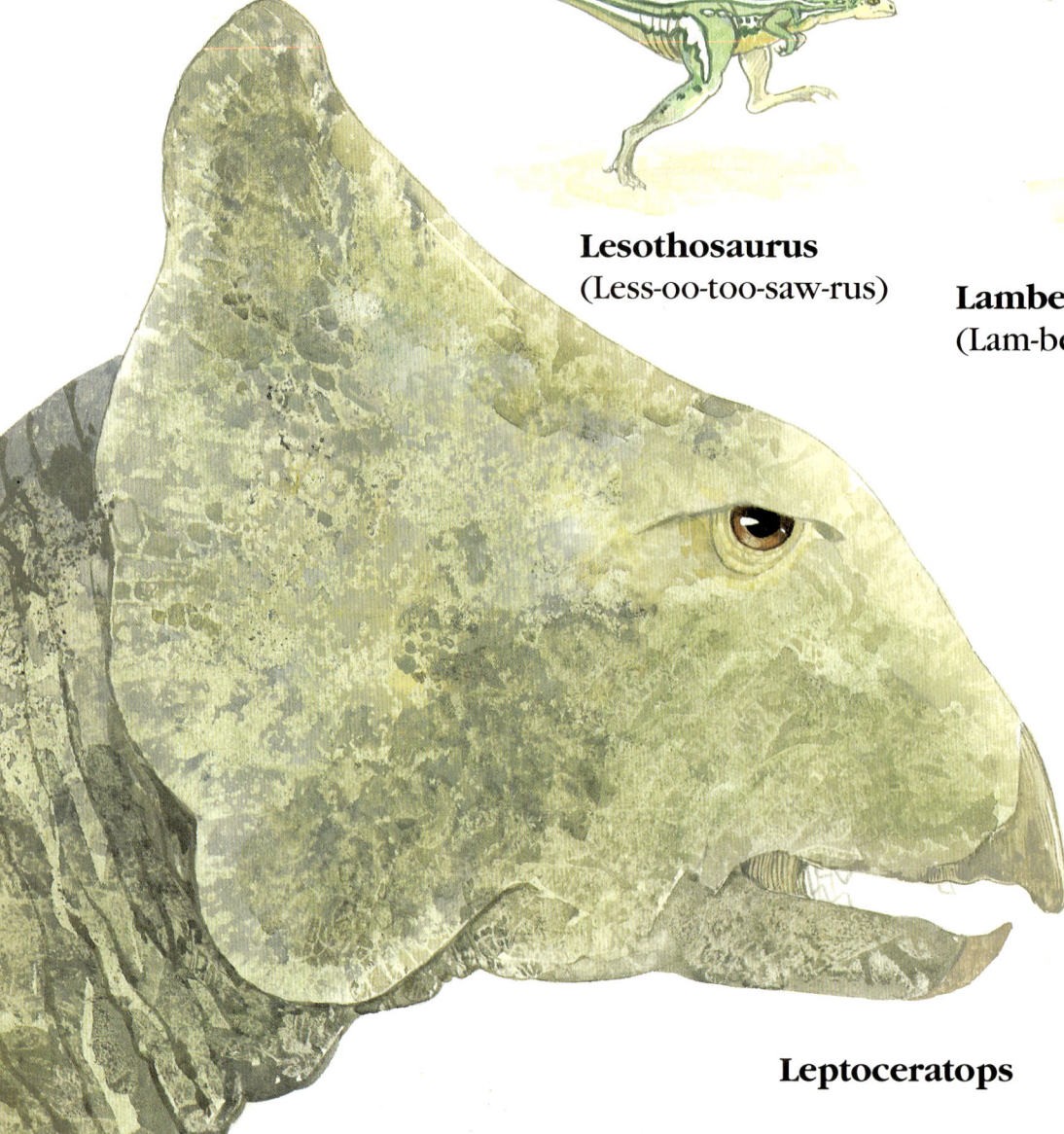

Leptoceratops

Lambeosaurus

Lesothosaurus

M

Megalosaurus
(Meg-al-owe-saw-rus)

26

Megalosaurus was the first dinosaur ever discovered. This huge meat-eater weighed 9 tonnes and walked on its strong back legs in search of food. It had sharp, rough-edged teeth and terrible claws on its feet. **Mamenchisaurus** was a very different creature. It was a slow, lumbering plant-eater which walked on all fours. This gentle giant had the longest neck of any animal. It was 10 metres long.

Mamenchisaurus
(Mam-en-key-saw-rus)

N

Some plant-eating dinosaurs grew so large that they were too slow to escape from enemies. So some dinosaurs, like **Nodosaurus**, had thick, bony lumps and plates covering their bodies. These were like a suit of armour which no meat-eater could bite through. The armour was flexible, though, so the dinosaur could still move about.

Nodosaurus was a plant-eater and lived about 95 million years ago in North America. Its name means "lumpy lizard".

Dinosaur armour
Other armour-plated dinosaurs included **Palaeoscinus**, **Scutellosaurus** and **Pinacosaurus**. As well as bony plates, these dinosaurs had sharp spikes for extra protection. Pinacosaurus could also swing its club-like tail at enemies, injuring them badly.

Palaeoscinus (Pal-ee-owe-sky-nus)

28

Nodosaurus
(Nod-owe-saw-rus)

Scutellosaurus
(Skut-ell-owe-saw-rus)

Pinacosaurus
(Pee-nah-co-saw-rus)

29

O

Ornithomimus and its close relative, **Oviraptor**, lived about 70 million years ago. Like **Ornitholestes**, these dinosaurs stole and ate eggs from other dinosaurs' nests. They probably picked them up with their long, thin fingers and broke them open with their sharp mouths. The name Oviraptor means "egg-thief", and Ornitholestes means "bird robber". Luckily, all three could run fast if they saw the parents of the eggs coming.

Ornitholestes
(Ore-nith-owe-less-tees)

Ornithomimus
(Ore-nith-owe-my-mus)

Oviraptor
(Oh-veer-ap-tor)

P

The **Pachycephalosaurus** was an odd-looking dinosaur. The bone on the top of its head was 25 centimetres thick. Scientists think that these big-headed dinosaurs took part in head-butting contests. These contests would decide which dinosaur would be head of the herd. The Pachycephalosaurus lived 70 million years ago in North America. If you'd been around then, you may have heard the sound of their heads banging together!

Pachycephalosaurus
(Pack-ee-sef-al-owe-saw-rus)

Dinosaur heads

There were many dinosaurs with strangely-shaped heads. Here are some of them.

Parasaurolophus
(Para-saw-rol-owe-fus)

Protoceratops
(Pro-tow-serra-tops)

Psittacosaurus
(Sit-ah-co-saw-rus)

33

P, Q

No dinosaurs ever lived in the sea or sky, but they had close relatives who did. **Plesiosaurus** and **Pliosaurus** were large sea reptiles. Plesiosaurus was a slow swimmer but could twist its long neck round quickly to snap up fish. Pliosaurus had a more streamlined body and could swim fast.

Pterodactylus and **Quetzalcoatlus** were flying reptiles. Quetzalcoatlus was the size of a small aeroplane and the largest animal ever to fly.

Plesiosaurus
(Plea-see-owe-saw-rus)

Pteranodon
(Tair-ah-no-don)

Pterodactylus
(Tair-owe-dac-til-us)

Quetzalcoatlus
(Kwet-zal-coat-lus)

Pliosaurus
(Plea-owe-saw-rus)

R

Rhamphorhynchus
(Ram-for-ring-cus)

From about 195 to 70 million years ago, the skies were full of flying reptiles. **Rhamphorhynchus** had a long, furry body and large, leathery wings. At the end of its bony tail was a flap of skin. The reptile may have used this as a rudder to help it steer in the air. The name Rhamphorhynchus means "narrow beak". This describes the reptile's beak-like jaws.

S

There were lots of dinosaurs beginning with the letter "s". **Saltopus** and **Segisaurus** were tiny, fast runners. **Saurolophus** was a duck-billed dinosaur with a small crest on its head. **Silvisaurus** had a solid, bony shield on its back and spikes sticking out from its shoulders and tail.

Saurolophus
(Saw-rol-owe-fus)

Silvisaurus
(Sill-vee-saw-rus)

Segisaurus
(Seg-ee-saw-rus)

Saltopus
(Salt-owe-pus)

S

Spine dinosaurs

Spinosaurus had a huge sail on its back, made of spikes covered with skin. This dinosaur lived in Africa about 110 million years ago. It probably used its sail to cool its body down.

Ouranosaurus lived about 105 million years ago in hot West Africa. It probably cooled down by standing with its sail side on to a breeze.

Stegosaurus
(Steg-owe-saw-rus)

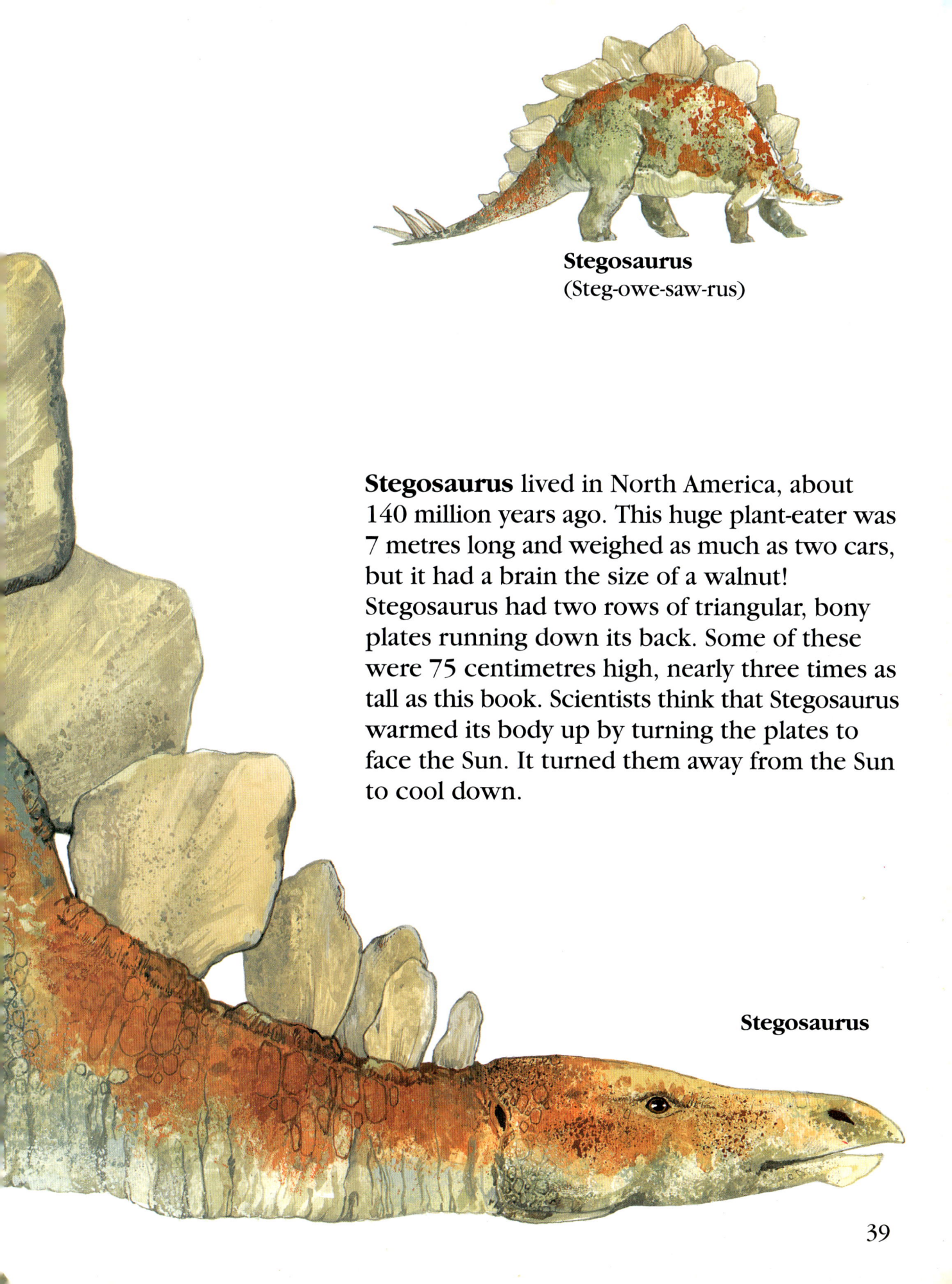

Stegosaurus lived in North America, about 140 million years ago. This huge plant-eater was 7 metres long and weighed as much as two cars, but it had a brain the size of a walnut! Stegosaurus had two rows of triangular, bony plates running down its back. Some of these were 75 centimetres high, nearly three times as tall as this book. Scientists think that Stegosaurus warmed its body up by turning the plates to face the Sun. It turned them away from the Sun to cool down.

Stegosaurus

T About 65 million years ago, the last of the dinosaurs lived on Earth. **Tyrannosaurus rex** was the largest meat-eater there has ever been. This monster stood 5 metres tall on its great clawed feet. It had terrible, dagger-like teeth which were 15 centimetres long. Even so, Tyrannosaurus rex may have thought twice about attacking **Torosaurus** or **Triceratops**. These plant-eaters had huge bony frills and fierce horns to protect themselves.

Triceratops
(Tri-sir-ah-tops)

Torosaurus
(Tor-row-saw-rus)

Tyrannosaurus rex
(Tie-ran-owe-saw-rus rex)

41

U, V, W

The word "dinosaur" comes from two Ancient Greek words meaning "terrible lizard". Most dinosaurs are named after their special features, or the place where their fossils were found. **Ultrasaurus** means "biggest lizard". It was only discovered about 10 years ago, but scientists think it may have been the biggest dinosaur of all. **Velociraptor** got its name because it was a very fast runner. **Wannanosaurus** is named after Wannan, the place in China where it was found.

Ultrasaurus
(Ul-tra-saw-rus)

Velociraptor
(Vel-owe-sir-ap-tor)

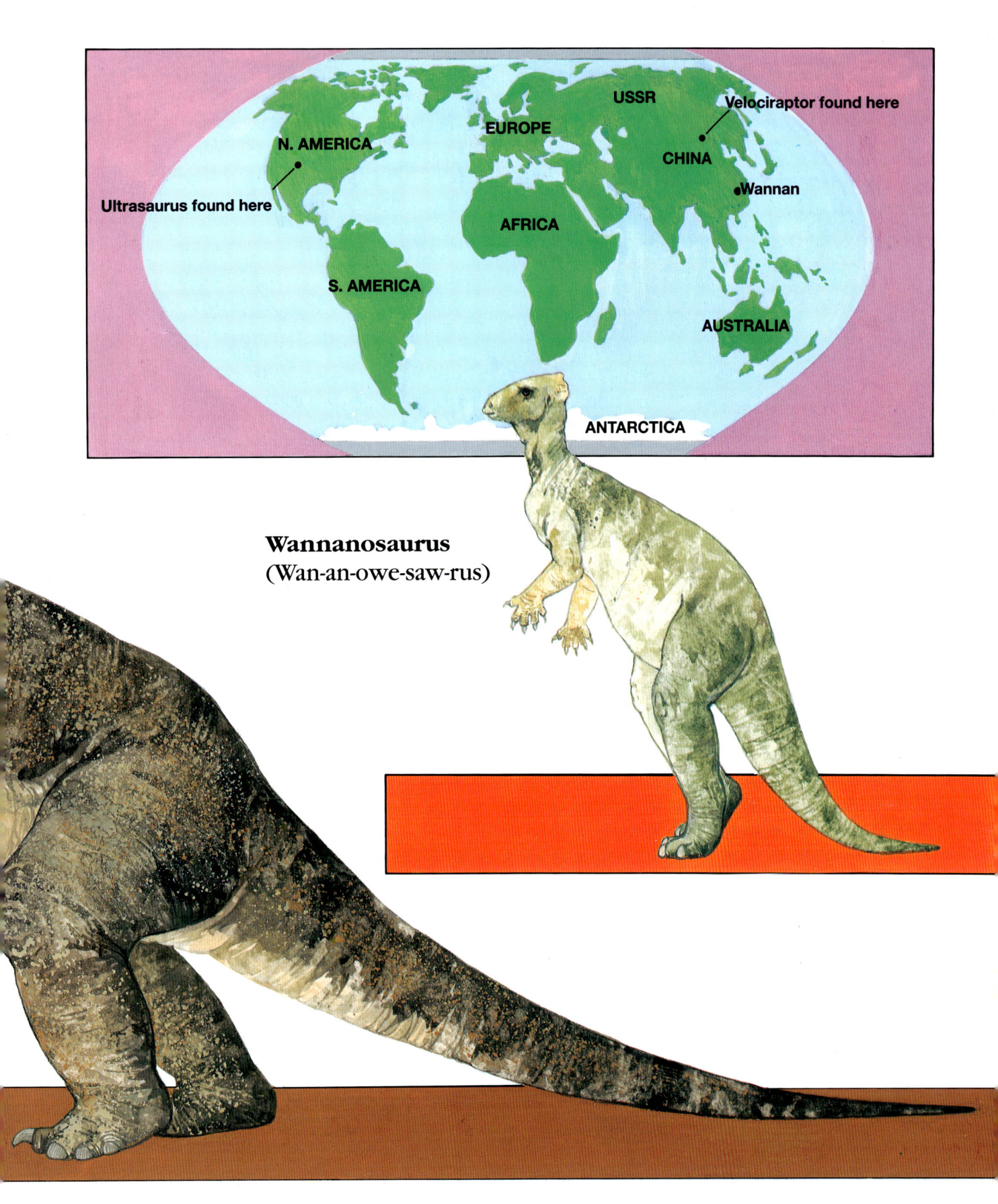

Wannanosaurus
(Wan-an-owe-saw-rus)

43

Y

Dinosaur fossils have been found all over the world, in deserts, in gravel pits and in cliffs. The first fossils were found over 300 years ago. Since then many important fossils of bones, teeth and even footprints have been found.

Yangchuanosaurus lived in China 145 million years ago. Its fossil skeleton was found in Yangchuan, East China in 1978.

Yangchuanosaurus
(Yan-chew-an-owe-saw-rus)

Yangchuanosaurus was a powerful hunter. Its skeleton is now on display in Beipei Museum, China.

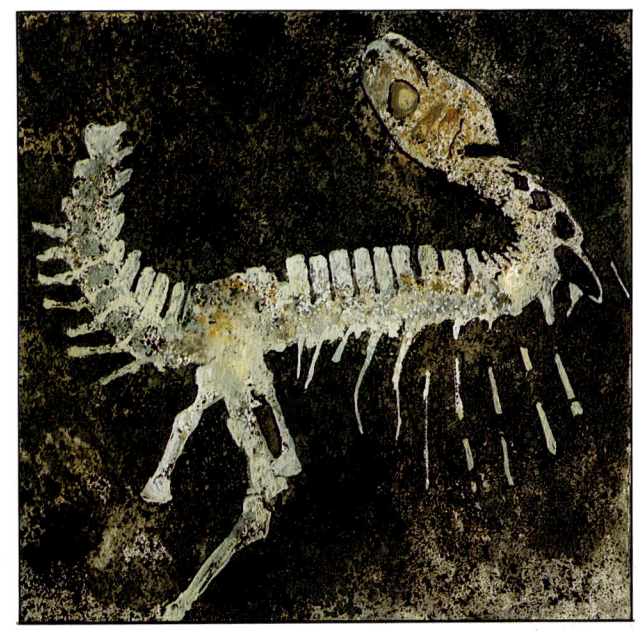

Z

Dinosaur experts are called **palaeontologists** (pale-ee-en-toll-owe-jists). They remove the fossils carefully from the rock and number and record each piece. Very fragile and crumbled bones may be wrapped in plaster casts, like a broken leg. The experts work out how old the dinosaurs are from the age of the rocks. Then they start the long job of fitting the jigsaw of bones together to make a skeleton.

Zephyrosaurus was a plant-eater which lived 120 million years ago. Its fossils were found in North America.

Zephyrosaurus
(Zeff-ear-owe-saw-rus)

INDEX

A
Albertosaurus 6
Anatosaurus 6
Archaeopteryx 6
armour 28

B
babies 22
bones 5, 44-5
Brachiosaurus 8, 10

C
Camarasaurus 9, 10
claws 27, 40
Coelophysis 10
Coelurus 10-11, 21
Compsognathus 10-11, 21
crests 24, 37
Cretaceous period 15

D
Diplodocus 12-13, 21

E
Edmontosaurus 14-15
eggs 4, 22, 30
Elasmosaurus 14-15
Euoplocephalus 15
Euskelosaurus 9

F
Fabrosaurus 16
feet 21, 40
flying 6, 34, 36
footprints 44
fossils 5, 18, 42, 44-5
frills 24, 40

G
Gallimimus 16-17

H
heads 10, 12, 24, 32-3, 37
herds 20, 32

Heterodontosaurus 18-19
horns 24, 40
Hypsilophodon 19

I
Iguanodon 20-1

J
Jubbulpuria 22

K
Kentrosaurus 22
Kronosaurus 22-3

L
Lambeosaurus 24-5
Leptoceratops 24-5
Lesothosaurus 24-5

M
Mamenchisaurus 26-7
Megalosaurus 26-7
mouths 24, 30

N
necks 9, 24, 27, 34
nests 22, 30
Nodosaurus 28-9

O
Ornitholestes 30-1
Ornithomimus 30-1
ostrich dinosaurs 16-17
Ouranosaurus 38
Oviraptor 30-1

P
Pachycephalosaurus 32-3
palaeontologists 45
Palaeoscinus 28
Parasaurolophus 33
Pinacosaurus 9
Plateosaurus 9
plates 15, 28, 38-9
Plesiosaurus 34-5
Pliosaurus 34-5
Protoceratops 33
Psittacosaurus 33

Pteranodon 35
Pterodactylus 34-5

Q
Quetzalcoatlus 34-5

R
Rhamphorhynchus 36

S
Saltopus 37
Saurolophus 37
scientists 18, 32, 39, 42
Scutellosaurus 28-9
Segisaurus 37
Silvisaurus 37
skeletons 20, 44-5
skulls 18
spikes 37, 38
spines 38
Spinosaurus 38
Stegosaurus 38-9
swimming 15, 22, 34

T
tails 12, 15, 16, 28, 36-7
teeth 5, 12, 18-19, 27, 36, 44
Torosaurus 40
Triceratops 40
Tyrannosaurus rex 40-1

U
Ultrasaurus 42-3

V
Velociraptor 42-3

W
Wannanosaurus 42-3
wings 36

Y
Yangchuanosaurus 44

Z
Zephyrosaurus 45